A PENOLOGICAL REVIEW OF INDIAN LAWS CRIMINALISING OBSCENITY

VOLUME 2, ISSUE 3 OF BRILLOPEDIA

SANGRAM JADHAV AND AYUSH GUPTA

Contents

Authors

Sangram Jadhav

Ayush Gupta

CHAPTER ONE

ABSTRACT

As beauty lies in the eyes of the beholder so does the vice of obscenity. The debate around laws criminalising "obscenity" predicates over differential notions of morality. But the ambiguous nature and interpretation of the term baffles the penal policy of any welfare State who continually struggles between advancing the interest of the public and protecting the liberty of its citizens. This paper seeks to dwell upon this dichotomy while analysing the penal policy of India in dealing with the practice of 'obscenity' in light of the well recognised principles of the Indian judicial system. It is intended to ponder over two prominent questions, namely: (1) which penal policy of the State should India adopt to justify criminalisation of obscenity in the media, whether print, electronic or otherwise?, and; (2) whether public views on morality determine the extent of bodily autonomy an individual legitimately exercises? To answer these questions, the authors seek to expound upon various established liberty-limiting principles and jurisprudential approaches to deal with 'obscenity' while discussing and analysing the extant obscenity-related legal provisions in India using such principles as a guiding light vis-à-vis the prevailing standards determining obscenity on the pedestal of constitutional morality. Further, the paper also reflects on different approaches espoused by other liberal States in curbing the practice and propose likely solutions in terms of tweaking of penological approach and re-look over the extant penal policy of the State.

The paper argues that the use of constitutional morality as a guiding principle would assure the required consistency in law while shunning the risk of arbitrariness. Therefore, the penal policy of the State should be informed by the canons of constitutional morality which would help the State to achieve its twin ideals of public interest and individual liberty in the most efficacious manner. The judiciary also must ensure that constitutional morality reigns supreme in their judicial engagement and imagination and refrain from getting indulged into defining the precincts of morality. The courts should strike a balancing act in advancing the public interest through the force of constitutional morality and should not be swayed by popular perceptions of societal morality.

CHAPTER TWO

INTRODUCTION

"Art, morals and law's manacles on aesthetics are a sensitive subject where jurisprudence meets other social sciences and never goes alone to bark and bite because State made straight-jacket is an inhibitive prescription for a free country unless enlightened society actively participates in the administration of justice to aesthetics"

- VR Krishna Iyer[1]

Criminal law provides a mechanism wherein the rights and liberties of an individual is pitted against the might of the State. The fundamental object of criminal law is not only to protect and to conserve the safety and security of personal rights but also to protect and guard public morals and public decency through the machinery of the State. Indian laws proscribe 'obscenity' and make its practice punishable under the extant laws of the land. However, the rule punishing the act of obscenity has always been fraught with controversies and ambiguities. The issue arises right from its definition which doesn't find place in any Indian statute book. There is no clear definition of what is indecent enough to warrant a criminal penalty. In a recent case that caught the public eye, actor and model MilindSoman was arrested for his allegedly obscene acts on a social media website. He posted a photograph in which he was seen sprinting naked on a beach in Goa. The photograph didn't go down well with some people to the extent that an FIR was lodged against Soman under §294 of the Indian Penal Code, 1860, and the applicable provisions of Information Technology Act, 2000. If at all this incident has done anything, it has resurrected the old debate on the criminalisation of obscenity, esp. in the world of electronic media, and the penological principles which should guide the State for punishing the perpetrator of this peculiar and undefined offence.

The word 'obscenity' is not defined under any Indian statute book. Cambridge Dictionary define it as anything "offensive, rude, or shocking, usually because of being too obviously related to sex or showing sex."[2] Merriam Webster Dictionary interprets it as anything (1) disgusting to the senses: Repulsive; 2(a) abhorrent to morality or virtue specifically: designed to incite to lust or depravity..... the dance often becomes flagrantly obscene and definitely provocative.....- Margaret Mead, (b) containing or being language regarded as taboo in polite usage obscene lyrics obscene literature, (c) repulsive by reason of crass disregard of moral or ethical principles an obscene misuse of power, (d) so excessive as to be offensive obscene wealth obscene waste."[3]

Soman's case reminds us of the famous late-19th Century AmilMitra's novel "Prajapati" which was castigated as being vulgar (inclusion of kissing scenes) and was seen to portend "obscene" depiction of love on the charge of it being morally depraved and debased and capable of encouraging the readers of any age to lasciviousness.[4] In a similar vein, critics accused Oscar Wilde's novel "The Picture of Dorian Gray" of being lewd because it included allusions to homosexuality. Sadat HasanManto's "trials and tribulations," wherein he wrote about "sex and lust, alcoholics and prostitutes, and was charged with obscenity six times,"[5] seem to be significant to the debate.

As beauty lies in the eyes of the beholder so does the vice of obscenity. The debate around laws criminalising obscenity predicates over differential notions of morality, especially between the moral perceptions of "literary elite" and the "average readers." This led Wilde to make the famous remark in the 1891 edition of his book that *there is no such thing as a moral or an immoral book. Books are well written, or badly written.*"[6] Every person presents his point of view respecting the essence of obscenity in his own way. It is sometimes termed as the "subversion of accepted standards of sexual morality",[7] the "individual or communal feelings of indignation",[8] the "leer of the sensualist",[9] or the "community sense of shame at the exposure of sexual or excremental matters."[10] Like India, several countries impose restrictions on circulation of obscene material. However, the vacillating standards to determine obscenity have often invited opprobrium on such standards being brandished as a tool for "cultural regulation

[1]Raj Kapoor v State, AIR 1980 SC 258

[2]VallabhaneniVamsi Mohan vs. State of Andhra Pradesh and Ors. (03.12.2019 - APHC) : MANU/AP/0350/2019

[3]*Ibid*

[4]Samaresh Bose vsAmal Mitra,1986 AIR 967: *In one of the passages of the novel, a person is shown to have taken his paramour out to show the sights of the city of Bombay but instead takes her to a picture where after the lights go off, seeing a soldier and his paramour in front kissing.*

[5]Osama Siddique, Capturing Obscenity: The Trials and Tribulations of SaadatHasanManto, 5 NNJLSR 15, 22 (2014).

[6] Emily Temple, A Close Reading of the 'Censored' Passages of The Picture of Dorian Gray (Dec. 27,2020,6:15PM),https://lithub.com/a-close-reading-of-the-originally-censored-passages-of-the-pictureof-dorian-gray

[7]Lockhart and McClure, Literature, The Law of Obscenity and the Constitution, 38 Minn. L. Rev. 295, 333 (1954) cited in Richard G. Fox, Obscenity, 12 Alberta L. Rev. 172, 173 (1974).

[8]MARCUSE, OBSCENE: THE HISTORY OF INDIGNATION 11 (1965) cited in Richard G. Fox, Obscenity, 12 Alberta L. Rev. 172, 173 (1974).

[9]U.S. v. One Book Called "Ulysses", 5 F. Supp. 182, 183 (1933).

[10]U.S. v. Kennerley, 209 Fed. 119, 121 (1913).

CHAPTER THREE

LIBERTY-LIMITING PRINCIPLES AND ITS APPLICATION ON CRIMINALISING OBSCENITY

The pre-constitutional Indian Penal Code of 1860 did not define 'obscenity' in any way. In the absence of a description, Justice Cockburn's test in R. v. Hicklin[1] applied. "Whether the material charged as obscene has the propensity to deprave and corrupt those whose minds are open to such immoral influences and into whose hands a publication of this type could fall..."[2] was the test. The matter was deemed 'obscene' if any aspect of it could be represented as depraved and corrupting the mind of the viewer to the satisfaction of the judges.

To determine which principle of criminalization appears to better explain the criminalization of obscenity in print and electronic media, all four standards must be tested to see whether they form the basis of the crime. The word "liberty-limiting (or coercion-legitimizing)" can be traced back to Joel Feinberg's landmark work "The Moral Limits of the Criminal Law," which runs into four volumes. Be that as it may, the following are the four principles that restrict liberty[3]:

<u>Legal Moralism</u>

Criminal law is particularly important in discussions about the relationship between law and morality because of its oppressive existence, societal stigma associated with criminal liability, and fetters on human liberty imposed by criminal penalties[1]. This is where the importance of legal moralism emerges. The relationship between the legal component (law) and the moral component (conduct that counts as morally wrong) is known as *legalmoralism*. Prof. HLA Hart invented the phrase in response to Lord Devlin in his book "Law, Liberty, and Morality."[2] The immediate context of the 1957 Wolfenden Committee's Report[3], which defended a particular conception of the role of criminal law and also declared that "law does not concern itself with immorality as such[4]," formed the contours of the debate that led to the acceptance of legal moralism as a liberty-limiting principle. This debate eventually devolved into a discussion of sexuality and morality.

Lord Devlin was a strong supporter of legal moralism. He believes that criminality should be attached to actions that demand it based on the moral convictions of "right-minded" individuals[5]. A "grossly immoral" act that elicits universal condemnation, a combination of "intolerance, outrage, and disgust," should be criminalised. He claims that public morality is the foundation of every human society, and that the primary role of law, especially criminal law, must be to preserve this foundation[6]. The state of public opinion decides whether a specific act can be criminalised by using legal force in the public interest. The common law jury ideal, also known as the "man in the jury-box," appears to be the adequate norm for deciding existing morality. According to Devlin, if vices are not suppressed, society would collapse[7]. A contemporary case of that time bolstered his argument[8]. He believes that the amount of damage done is unimportant. Instead of seeking any "real morality" to create a better society, Devlin argued that law should impose "positive morality" to maintain a stronger society.

Hart disagreed with Devlin's point of view. Hart distinguished between morality that is constructive and morality that is critical. He defined positive morality as "morality that is actually embraced and shared by a given social community," whereas critical morality is defined as "moral values used in the critique of actual social institutions, including positive morality."[9] Positive morality, on the other hand, is concerned with society's dominant moral convictions, whereas critical morality is concerned with what is objectively morally necessary based on an individual's best judgement. Based on this distinction, positive morality will settle for nothing less than the actual immorality of homosexuality for its criminalization, while vital legal morality will settle for nothing less than the actual immorality of homosexuality for its criminalization[10]. Both of these moral conceptions, according to Hart, must be accounted for. As a result, Hart acknowledges that morality is necessary for society's survival. He refers to these as "universal principles."[11] .

These offences are "egregious and willful violations of the moral law...extremely harmful to society[12]." Devlin wanted to impose "real public morality," not some "true morality.[13]" Hart, on the other hand, was adamant that universal principles should not be applied simply because they were universally held, regardless of their substance. Devlin, he claims, has not taken into account shifts in social mores[14].

This principle seeks to prohibit actions that are intrinsically unethical, even though they are not harmful or offensive. Morals are ingrained in culture. They are embodied in the society's collective conscience, and if this morality is removed, the society will inevitably disintegrate[15]

On the basis of above discussion, If we examine the language used 'It is lascivious or appeals to the prurient interest, or if the overall effect of any of its items is to appear to deprave and corrupt individual, who are likely, having regard to all relevant circumstances, to read, see, or hear the matter contained or embodied in it' according to §292 and 293 of the IPC. §2(C) of the Indecent Representation of Women (Prohibition) Act, 1986 represents legal moralism by banning any matter from entering the public domain that is "likely to deprave, corrupt, or harm the public morality or morals." The IT Act of 2000, §67, 67A, and 67B, which criminalise obscenity in electronic media, also refer to "lascivious content appealing to prurient interest" and "sexually explicit act".

Harm Principle

This theory is synonymous with John Stuart Mill's seminal work, "On Liberty." In that work, he introduced this theory and proposed that the imposition of criminal liability by the state can be justified only when an individual's conduct has the potential to cause danger or injury to another person[1]. The theory was developed to regulate the individual-society relationship. Mill, a proponent of liberty, claims that the only acts for which a society should hold a person responsible are those that cause harm to others. This is best exemplified in his prose, where he claims that "freedom is, by right, absolute." The person has sovereign authority over himself, his own body and mind[2]. The Millian notion of liberty would not justify the exercise of coercive power of the State to prevent an individual from causing moral harm to himself. Mill says that the good of the individual concerned "whether physical or moral, is not a sufficient warrant".[3] When coercion is used to discourage specific actions, the behaviour to be avoided "must be determined to cause harm to someone else[4]." Mill, on the other hand, gives no description of the term "harm." Albeit, lexically speaking, the word can be interpreted to mean, among others, "adverse effect on 'interests,' or 'injury', 'hurt' or anything evil or a wrong[5] As can be shown, Mill's viewpoint prioritises individual autonomy or the ability to make decisions, but it also places limitations on it in order to protect the interests of those in society. On these lines, we can say that if a clear connection can be formed between criminalisedbehaviour and societal harm, this principle would apply. A review of case law on the issue of obscenity reveals that moral harm to the individual is prioritised above any physical harm caused by the accused's actions. In India, the connection between criminalizing obscenity and causing physical harm to any person has yet to be conclusively investigated or established.

Offense Principle

The offence principle of criminalization places the State in charge of preventing offensive behaviour. Feinberg states that criminalization would be "an efficient way of preventing serious crime (as opposed to injury or harm) to individuals other than the actor" and that it would be "the most effective means of ending social regulation in the given circumstances."[1] Feinberg constructs a thought-experiment based on a fictional scenario called "A Ride in a Bus," in which he creates thirty-one scenes of varying degrees of hated mental state severity.

These scenes can be divided into six groups: Shock to moral, religious, or patriotic sensibilities; Affronts to the senses; Disgust and revulsion; Fear, indignation, humiliation, and anger; Shame, embarrassment (including vicarious embarrassment), and anxiety; Annoyance, boredom, and frustration; and (from empty threats, insults, mockery, flaunting, or taunting).[2] Feinberg's fundamental question is whether there are any human encounters that, while innocuous in isolation, are so unpleasant that legal immunity from them can be sought, even at the expense of other people's freedom[3]. When viewed from a legislative standpoint, these "offended states" are essentially offensive annoyances. These factors make it impossible for anyone to enjoy their time in a place where they "cannot reasonably be expected to leave in the circumstances."[4] The term "offense" is defined both in a general and normative sense. In the general sense, it refers to "any or all of a miscellany of disliked mental states (disgust, shame, hurt, anxiety, etc.)"[5]. In the normative sense, it refers to the abovementioned states "only when caused by the wrongful (right-violating) conduct of others"[6] The offence theory, as described by Feinberg, is only concerned with the second meaning of offence. The crime must be committed wrongfully by another person, according to the theory. The victim, on the other hand, does not have to feel wronged[7]. As a result, it would be an offense if these disliked states of mind are instilled in another person without reason or excuse, with or without the victim feeling resentful.

If we examine §292 and 293 of IPC, it will be found that these sections talk about the capacity of the obscene matter to "deprave and corrupt", and not to "shock or disgust." The same happens to be the thinking behind §67 of the IT Act. However, the Indecent Representation of Women (Prohibition) Act, 1986 in part incorporates the offense principle when §2 (c) defines indecent representation of women as the "depiction of figure of women...in such a way as to have the effect of being indecent or derogatory or denigrating to women." §294 of IPC also talks about "annoyance caused to others" by an obscene act in public.

However, the author believes that this emotional state is caused by society's perception of an individual's actions as inherently immoral. The moral evaluation of the action influences the decision on its offensiveness.

Legal Paternalism

As the name implies, paternalism is concerned with the State acting as a parent to the individual, teaching him to stay away from things that have the potential to hurt him. HLA Hart modifies Mill's harm theory marginally in 'Law, Liberty, and Morality', claiming that there might be times when an individual's judgement is clouded either by transient desires or other predicaments. Consent is granted without proper consideration or understanding of the implications in this situation. Individuals should be protected from injuring themselves in this way by the State[1]. Paternalism, according to Danny Scoccia, is an "attempt to compel people to behave in ways that will help them, or to refrain from acting in ways that will hurt them[2]." As a result, State coercion is justified in order to discourage individuals from injuring themselves. This may be due to a benevolent regard for the peoples' well-being. Individual autonomy is therefore hampered by State paternalism, which criminalises such actions in order to protect people from self-inflicted harm.

The theory of legal paternalism, according to Feinberg, directs people for their own benefit "whether they like it or not." He compares government interference in citizen's lives to parents intervening in their children's lives on the grounds that they know best what is best for their children. In the same way, the State becomes the permanent protector of the individual's rights, knowing them better than the people do[3]. As a result, the State becomes the "parent of last resort[4]," as Feinberg puts it.

There are two forms of paternalism:-

A. Hard paternalism is when the government uses force to limit an individual's autonomy. Examples of this kind of practice can be found in the NDPS Act.

B. Soft paternalism is where no force is used and the individual's viewpoint is swayed in order to get him to behave in a way that will benefit him. The statutory warning on a cigarette pack is a classic example of this kind of paternalism.

Individual autonomy supporters have criticised the State for forcing on people a "concept of good life" that they do not find attractive enough. It is a violation of individuals' autonomy, according to them, because they have the freedom to choose what constitutes a "normal life" for them. Proponents of legal paternalism claim that, in some situations, paternalism tends to maximise individual liberty in the long run, i.e., an individual's ability to behave rationally as a human being[5].

The harm to the seller or producer of obscene content has not been considered in laws dealing[6] with the criminalization of obscenity in print and electronic media. However, paternalistic undertones of the penal policy can be culled out from the Court's interpretation in *RanjitUdeshi case*[7] and attempts by obscenity-regulating legislation to prevent individuals from "depravity" and corruption. Thus, legal moralism and legal paternalism are the values that best explain the criminalization of obscenity in print and electronic media. The reasons to support this hypothesis will be provided in the next section.

[1] Christine Pierce, Hart on Paternalism, 35 (6) Oxford Academic Analysis 205, 205 (1975)

[2] Danny Scoccia, In Defense of Hard Paternalism, 27 (4) Law and Philosophy 351, 352 (2008)

[3] Joel Feinberg, Legal Paternalism, 1 (1) Canadian Journal of Philosophy 105, 105 (1971)

[4] JOEL FEINBERG, HARM TO SELF 6 (1989)

[5]Danny Scoccia, In Defense of Hard Paternalism, 27 (4) Law and Philosophy 351, 355 (2008).

[6]§ 292, 293 and 294 of the Indian Penal Code; Section 67 of the Information and Technology Act of 2000; and §s 2(c), 3 and 4 of the Indecent Representation of Women Prohibition Act of 1986, the Cable Television Network Regulation Act of 1995 makes it illegal to broadcast obscene content on television.

[7]AIR 1965 SC 881. The case was brought by a bookseller who was charged with obscenity under the Indian Penal Code for selling an unexpurgated edition of the novel "Lady Chatterley's Lover," in which the author elaborated on the sexual intimacies of the protagonist. The case was dismissed

[1]JOEL FEINBERG, OFFENSE TO OTHERS xii (1985)

[2]*Ibid*

[3]*Ibid*

[4]*Ibid.*

[5]*Ibid*

[6]*Ibid*

[7]*Ibid*

[1]J.S. MILL, ON LIBERTY: COLLECTED WORKS OF JOHN STUART MILL, ED. J.M. ROBSON 22 (1977).

[2] JOHN STUART MILL, ON LIBERTY (1859), Stefan Collini, ed. (1989), chap. 1, cited in MICHAEL SANDEL, JUSTICE: WHAT'S THE RIGHT THING TO DO? 49 (2009).

[3]JOHN STUART MILL, ON LIBERTY (1859), Stefan Collini, ed. (1989), chap. 1., cited in MICHAEL SANDEL, JUSTICE: WHAT'S THE RIGHT THING TO DO? 49 (2009)

[4]R. REEVES, JOHN STUART MILL - VICTORIAN FIREBRAND 265 (2007) cited in Clare McGlynn and Ian Ward, Would John Stuart Mill have Regulated Pornography? , 41 (4) Journal of Law and Society 500, 505 (2014).

[5]*Ibid*

[1]Peter Cane, Taking Law Seriously: Starting Points of the Hart/Devlin Debate, 10 The Journal of Ethics 21, 40 (2006)

[2]HLA HART, LAW, LIBERTY AND MORALITY 6 (1963), cited in Peter Cane, Taking Law Seriously: Starting Points of the Hart/Devlin Debate, 10 The Journal of Ethics 21, 28 (2006)

[3] Report of the Committee on Homosexual Offences and Prostitution, 1957 (UK)

[4] *Ibid*, Paragraph 13.

[5] Immorality then, for the purpose of the law, is what every right-minded person is presumed to consider to be immoral (Devlin, 1963, p. 15) cited in Jens DamgaardThaysen, Defining Legal Moralism 16 (2) SATS 179, 195 (2015).

[6] M.D.A. FREEMAN, LLOYD'S INTRODUCTION TO JURISPRUDENCE 603 (2014).

[7] *Ibid*

[8] DPP v. Shaw. [1962] A.C. 74. It was held that courts are "custodians of the public morals" with "a residual power... to conserve not only the safety and order but also the moral welfare of the State"

[9] HLA HART, LAW, LIBERTY AND MORALITY, 20 (1963), cited in Peter Cane, Taking Law Seriously: Starting Points of the Hart/Devlin Debate, 10 The Journal of Ethics 21, 28 (2006)

[10] Jens DamgaardThaysen, Defining Legal Moralism 16 (2) SATS 179, 181 (2015).

[11] H.L.A. HART, THE CONCEPT OF LAW 193-200 (1994) cited in Jens DamgaardThaysen, Defining Legal Moralism 16 (2) SATS 179, 192 (2015)

[12] *Ibid*

[13] A. R. Blackshield, The Hart Devlin Controversy in 1965, 5 Sydney Law Review 441, 445 (1967)

[14] Peter Cane, Taking Law Seriously: Starting Points of the Hart/Devlin Debate, 10 The Journal of Ethics 21, 24 (2006)

[15] PATRICK DEVLIN, THE ENFORCEMENT OF MORALS 89 (1965) cited in A. R. Blackshield, The Hart Devlin Controversy in 1965, 5 Sydney Law Review 441, 450 (1967): "Morality, if not 'a single seamless web', is at any rate 'a web of beliefs rather than a number of unconnected ones' and if for want of legal protection any part of it is weakened, or seen to be flouted with immunity, the popular conviction sustaining the whole web may be undermined. If this happens, society itself may be threatened. For society is 'a community of ideas', including moral ideas; morality 'is built into the house in which we live and could not be removed without bringing it down."

[1] [1868] 3 L.R. (QB) 360

[2] *Ibid*

[3] JOEL FEINBERG, HARM TO OTHERS 83-90 (1987)

CHAPTER FOUR

WHAT DRIVES THE INDIAN PENAL POLICY?

Being a culture known for its 'moral' and dogmatic origins, India was in a moral quandary on variegated liberal notions borrowed from occidental constitutions. With commencement of the constitution came a case challenging the constitutionality of §292 IPC in *RanjitUdeshi v. State of Maharashtra*[1] on the ground of being contrary to the freedom of speech & expression. The apex court upheld the impugned provision holding it a reasonable restriction on the exercise of the said freedom in the interest of public decency and morality.[2]

The Court followed Hicklin'stest and considered its application justified owing to its emphasis on potentiality of the impugned provision to deprave and corrupt by immoral influences.[3] It, however, modified the application of the test to the extent that its application in India could not be said to hold ground on stray excerpts of obscene connotations but should be judged on the altar of community standards without a preponderating social purpose or profit.[4]

Enforcement of Morality

The Hart-Devlin debate continues to be of cardinal importance in the domain of legal moralism. Upholding §292 of the Penal Code, the Court held the restrictions reasonable and found them well in the interest of public decency and morality as required by the Constitution thereby regarding moralism to be the deciding factor.[5] The judges noted that obscenity appeals or has a tendency to appeal "to the carnal side of human nature" [6] and no protection of free speech exists for "obscenity without a preponderance of social purpose or profit."[7]. A material is deemed obscene under §292 if it is lascivious or appeals to the prurient interest, or if the overall effect of any of its products is to deprave and corrupt people who are likely to read, see, or hear the matter contained or embodied in it. §2(c) of Indecent Representation of Women (Prohibition) Act, 1986, also reflects legal moralism by prohibiting any matter which is "likely to deprave, corrupt or injure the public morality or morals" from entering the public domain. §s 67, 67A and 67B in IT Act, 2000 which criminalize publishing or transmitting obscene material in electronic media also talk in terms of "lascivious material appealing to prurient interest" and "sexually explicit act." The language of the provisions and the test for obscenity followed in the said legal provisions indicate - what is obscene (and hence, worthy of criminalisation)? It is determined on the basis of prevailing notions of morality and decency in the society. On closer analysis, it is found that the Court had advocated curbs on freedom of speech and expression in the interest of contemporary society. Public decency and morality should direct these restrictions. This viewpoint is similar to Lord Devlin's belief that humanity has the right to defend itself against something that threatens its moral convictions. The criterion for deciding it was to be that of "the man in the jury box," which seems to be the "interest of contemporary society," according to the Court in *Udeshi*. A public showing of this interest in sexual affairs has been deemed intrinsically unethical by society because it goes against society's sexual mores. It is commonly believed that social institutions of marriage and family might collapse by the presence of obscene material as the latter has the potential to change the social perception about sex and relationship for which it is widely believed that India is not for.[8]

The desire to preserve the social fabric militates against the inclusion of obscene content in the public domain, and this cultural interest appears to direct the criminalization of obscenity. The use of criminal penalties to avoid the reshaping of society's moral contours toward public expectation, as well as the need to instil a proper attitude against obscenity[9], can be contained in the state's penal policy. In *SukantaHaldar v. State*[10], the court opined that obscene matters tend to increase "sex impulse which leads to sexually impure and lustful thoughts". It can thus be said that what is criminalised is the conduct that scatologically influence the discourse of a 'civilised' society and not the conduct which harms another or entail an offensive mental reaction in another person[11]

Protection from Depravity

A careful examination of court's observation in *Udeshi* reveal that law proscribing obscenity was concerned not only with moralism but extend to insulating society from immoral influences causing depravity and corruption in the social landscape[12], and the intention of law is to protect "not those who can protect themselves but those whose prurient minds take delight and seek sexual pleasure from erotic writings."[13] The obscenity laws are concerned more towards precluding individual/social morality from getting degenerated. [14] This importance the Court ascribes to "protection" evinces that the court was conscious of the harm of moral depravity and corruption of an individual. This makes the provision more of a kind that satisfies the attributes of legal paternalism as an instrument of State's penal policy. The terms used by the legislature in §292 and §293 of the IPC further support this. The aim of criminalising obscene content, according to the second limb of §292, is to prevent the mind of the person who is likely to see, hear, or read it from being depraved or corrupted. The court believes that "moral depravity and corruption" are harmful to individuals. When we examine obscenity laws to see what kind of paternalism they represent, we find that they adhere to the hard version of moral paternalism, in which the state uses coercion to preserve the individual's beliefs and improve their moral character in order to improve their well-being.[15] The state takes on the duty of strengthening the moral fabric of society by allowing or prohibiting such actions that, in the State's opinion, will improve a person's moral character and prevent him from harming himself morally. A review of obscenity case law decided after *Udeshi* is required to demonstrate that, despite significant changes in the test for defining obscenity, the cultural standards test still reigns supreme. This cultural norm represents the societal consensus on the moral correctness of every action. The concepts established after *Udeshi* will be discussed in the following section.

[1]*Ibid*
[2]*Ibid*
[3]*Ibid*
[4]*Ibid*
[5]*Ibid*

[6] RanjitUdeshi v. State Maharashtra, AIR 1965 SC 881

[7] *Ibid*

[8] Gautam Bhatia, RanjitUdeshi – II: The Enforcement of Morals (Dec. 25, 2020, 7:50 PM), https://indconlawphil.wordpress.com/2013/08/05/ranjit-udeshi-and-the-enforcement-of-morals/

[9] M. Cathleen Kaveny, Obscenity, Communal Values, and the Law: Joel Feinberg and the Failure of Liberalism, 9 The Annual of the Society of Christian Ethics 93, 97 (1989)

[10] AIR 1952 Cal. 214

[11] This point can also be backed up by Henkin, who claims that "obscenity laws are not primarily motivated by any belief that obscene materials inspire sexual offences." Obscenity laws, on the other hand, are founded on conventional conceptions of government accountability for communal and individual decency and morality, which are rooted in this country's religious antecedents.``L. Henkin, Morals and the constitution-The sin of obscenity, 63 Column L.R. 391, 391 (1963)

[12] RanjitUdeshi v. State Maharashtra, AIR 1965 SC 881, ¶19.

[13] RanjitUdeshi v. State Maharashtra, AIR 1965 SC 881, ¶26

[14] Gautam Bhatia, RanjitUdeshi – III: Paternalism and the Meaning of "Morality" (Dec. 26, 2020, 8:15 PM),https://indconlawphil.wordpress.com/2013/08/06/ranjit-udeshi-paternalism-and-the-meaning-of-morality/

[15] Dworkin,"Paternalism",(Dec.26,2020,9:25M)https://plato.stanford.edu/archives/fall2020/entries/paternalis

CHAPTER FIVE

JUDICIAL TRAJECTORY AFTER UDESHI

Indian Courts have restrained in placing reliance on one straight-jacket test for determining the charge of obscenity, and instead decided to evolve tests based on the facts and circumstances of the case.[1] The Court in *AnandPatwardhan*[2] adopted the "contemporary community standards" test as laid down in *Miller v. California* by the US Supreme Court[3]. This shifted the judicial focus in deciding matters pertaining to obscenity to social mores prevailing at a particular point of time. In *Ajay Goswami*[4], "community-based standard'[5] test was ignored and dubbed redundant, and "Responsible Reader Test" was propounded where the culpability hinges on the impact of sexually explicit content on minors.

Taking cue from a US case[6] where a category of material was pointed out which albeit unsuitable for the children, was acceptable to adults and could not be permitted to be withdrawn from public domain only for protecting children from any potential harm caused by this material. Ascribing importance to the norms of society, the court opined that "regard must be had to contemporary mores and national standards."[7]The argument that either the art must be preponderating to reduce obscenity to triviality, or the impact of obscenity must be trivial enough to be ignored guides judicial meanderings in the thickets of obscenity and art.[8]

In *K. A. Abbas,*[9] The Supreme Court made a distinction between "Sex" and "Obscenity," stating that it would be incorrect to regard nudity and sex as inherently pornographic, indecent, or immoral. There had to be a line drawn where "The average moral man" is embarrassed by the "naked image of life without the redeeming touch of art, genius, or social value."[10]

Further safeguards were introduced in *Samaresh Bose*[11], where the test for the most likely audience was laid out "The judge should strive to put himself in the author's shoes and consider what the author is attempting to convey," the Court said. Then he should speculate about the effect it could have on readers of all ages, and critically judge the book as a whole using his judicial mind."[12] It was also observed that the "social outlook of the people who are generally expected to read the book"[13] shapes, to a large extent, the contours to contest the charge of obscenity. The "standards of morality of contemporary society in different countries" determines what is considered as obscene in that jurisdiction.

In *Aveek Sarkar,*[14] it was held that a material cannot be called obscene "unless it has the tendency to arouse feelings or revealing an overt sexual desire". This has to be judged from the "point of view of an average person."[15] This reasoning goes on the lines of the "man in the jury box" standard as propounded by Devlin.

All these judicial tests are different means to achieve the same end of prevention of disintegration of society ostensibly caused by the moral vices of individuals in society. The fear of "corruption" and "moral harm" speaks for moral paternalism guiding the penal policy of the state to prevent the society from flagellating itself.

All subsequent changes to Hicklin's test do not significantly alter the rules, and obscenity is still described in terms of sexual explicitness, which is morally repugnant by social standards. As a result, a closer examination of both of these cases reveals that judicial interpretation has often sided with legal moralism and paternalism as guiding principles in the criminalization of obscenity.

[1] This is consistent with the Supreme Court's statement that "there can be no universal test of obscenity" and that "each case must be decided on its own facts."" See, Ranjit D. Udeshi v. State of Maharashtra, AIR 1965 SC 881.

[2] (2006) 8 SCC 433. Respondent's documentary film "Father, Son, and Holy War," which dealt with issues of gender and religious conflict, was rejected by Doordarshan. The Court ruled that the entire film conveyed a serious message in the current sense, and Doordarshan was ordered to display it.

[3] 413 U.S. 15 (1973).

[4] (2007) 1 SCC 143.

[5] Miller vs. California, 413 U.S. 15 (1973)

[6] Alfred E. Butler v. State of Michigan, 1 LED 2d 412 [The Supreme Court held that "The state claims that by restricting the general public's access to books that are not too challenging for grown men and women in

order to protect juvenile innocence, it is acting in the public interest..”

[7](2007) 1 SCC 143, 169.

[8]Ranjit D. Udeshi v. State of Maharashtra, AIR 1965 SC 881, 889

[9] (1970) 2 SCC 780.The director tried to depict the stark contrast between the lives of rich and poor people in these cities in a documentary titled "A Tale of Four Cities." It featured scenes from red-light districts as well as oblique sexual references. If these scenes were omitted from the film, a 'U' certificate will be given. The constitutionality of the pre-censorship laws was questioned by the petitioner.These laws were upheld as lawful, with the caveat that sexually explicit scenes would not be subject to censorship, and that value judgments on how the theme was handled should be taken into account.

[10]*Ibid*

[11](1985) 4 SCC 289.The novel "Prajapati," which included references to kissing, body descriptions, and suggestive references to sexual intercourse, was deemed obscene. However, it was deemed “not obscene” in light of the test proposed.

[12]*Ibid*

[13]*Ibid*

[14]4(2014) 4 SCC 257. Boris Becker and his wife were photographed naked and released in the AnandbazarPatrika, which was deemed obscene. The Court, on the other hand, held that the photograph’s message and the background in which it was written should be considered. The image was deemed to be “not obscene.”

[15]*Ibid*

CHAPTER SIX

A GLANCE OVER OTHER LIBERAL JURISDICTIONS

In the world of globalisation where factors such as social, economic, cultural, political of one State are intermingled and cause great influence on the moral and ethical character of the other State, it is incumbent, in light of the topic of this discussion, to understand perspectives of different jurisdictions qua the issue of obscenity.

In United Kingdom, the factor taken into account to decide on the culpability of obscenity is the potential effect of the impugned material on persons likely to come into its contact so as to deprave and corrupt them[1]. Therefore, it can be said that the UK follows the philosophical approach of Legal moralism and paternalism as a policy of State's penal policy.

In USA, *Miller's* test[2] (as discussed above) is considered as a guiding penal policy of the State which evinces the moralist and paternalistic character of the State to deal with matters pertaining to obscenity

Canada penalises the depiction of explicit sex (with or without violence) that subjects the participants to degrading or dehumanizing treatment. The emphasis is not on "preserving morals" but on protecting the society from harm which "predisposes persons to act in an anti-social manner."[3] Therefore, it can verily be said that it follows the Harm Principle as a principle of State's penal policy.

South Africa emphasises on constitutionally- recognized harm. The legal position can be traced to *De Reuck v. DPP*[4], wherein the emphasis was on *violation of constitutionally-protected right to dignity*[5] which evinces the applicability of harm principle in the penal policy of the State.

Thus, it can verily be said that while Anglo-American approach draws its strength from the penological principles of legal moralism and paternalism and focuses on public morality, the approach in Canada and South Africa gives emphasis on harm, which is understood in the context of established constitutional values such as dignity and equality. Indian tests are closer to the Anglo-American model. The Canadian and South African approaches are in consonance with the case for constitutional morality, which is made out in the next section.

[1] §1, Obscene Publications Act, 1959. Derived from R. v. Hicklin, [1868] 3 L.R. (QB) 360.

[2] Miller vs. California, 413 U.S. 15 (1973) redefined the definition of obscenity from that of "utterly without socially redeeming value" to that which lacks "serious literary, artistic, political, or scientific value". It is now referred to as the three-prong standard or the Miller test. It deems a work as obscene '*if:*

a) By applying contemporary cultural expectations, the average citizen will conclude that the work appeals to the prurient interest as a whole.

b) The work portrays or defines sexual activity clearly described by the relevant state law in a patently offensive manner, contrary to contemporary community standards.

c) The work, as a whole, is of no literary, cultural, political, or scientific significance.'

[3] Donald Victor Butler v. Her Majesty the Queen and the Attorney General of Canada et al., 1992 S.C.R. 452 (1992) at 485.

[4] 2004(1) SA 406

[5] SOUTH AFRICA CONST, §10: It safeguards people's intrinsic dignity.

CHAPTER SEVEN

THROUGH THE PERSPECTIVE OF CONSTITUTIONAL MORALITY

The court recently ruled in *Indian Hotel and Restaurant Association v. State of Maharashtra*[1] that the concept of obscenity is culture and community-specific[2], and that the word is used in the legal sense to denote expressions that are contrary to the prevalent sexual morality[3]. Social morality is ephemeral, and if the law does not keep pace, it is up to the Court to use imaginative judicial interpretation to build a bridge between the past and the present. This gives the courts a lot of leeway in deciding what is and isn't obscene on the altar of constitutional morality.

The laws against obscenity, according to Henkin, are based on conventional conceptions of morality and decency. As a result, the definition of obscenity is based on the "terms in which culture has framed it." He also sees a religious foundation in the origins of the crime, tracing the words "lascivious" and "prurient interest" to Christian notions of sexual morality. Any sex that isn't for the purpose of reproduction is considered a "original sin."[4] This idea was imported in the IPC. As a result, this moral interpretation tends to have religious roots.

It's worth noting that Hart and Dworkin aren't against enforcing morality, but they are in favour of establishing a high bar for what constitutes morality[5]. According to LatikaVashist, redefining the state's criminalization policies along the lines of constitutional morality will help address the problem of unprincipled criminalization[6], which can lead to "under-criminalization" or "overcriminalization"[7] This section takes this argument further in the context of obscenity laws.

Morality in today's Indian culture cannot be dismissed as a personal matter. However, the question of which definition of morality can be used to constrain human autonomy arises. The three conceptions of morality which could be used are- public morality, individual morality and constitutional morality. Lord Devlin's standard of "man in jury-box" is synonymous with public or popular morality. It refers to the society's viewpoints at any given point in time. If this definition of morality is adopted, it will become clear that mainstream morality has the capacity to morph into majoritarian morality. This majoritarian morality can then suffocate the minority's right to self-determination and, as a result, sovereignty. Using this viewpoint, free expression will be subject to majoritarian notions of right and wrong. In the case of Naz Foundation v. NCT[8], this was realised. In a pluralistic society like India, determining what constitutes obscenity in the eyes of the community becomes extremely difficult, and relying on a single moral opinion can stifle the voices of dissenting minorities and lead to restrictions on their freedom of speech on arbitrary grounds. Individual morality is based on individualistic values and emphasises autonomy. This kind of morality, on the other hand, would make regulating obscene matter exceedingly difficult because it will jeopardise uniformity in obscene matter regulation standards.

Constitutional morality is distinct from both popular and individual morality. It represents a dedication to the fundamental political and moral philosophy that underpins our Constitution. It forbids any act that smacks of arbitrariness[9]. Constitutional morality has "inherent elements in the constitutional norms and conscience of the Constitution[10].

The standard for obscenity has become outmoded in the digital age, according to the *Ajay Goswami case*[11]. In terms of constitutional morality, this necessitates a rethinking. Even the tiniest segment of society has the right to have different tastes and desires as long as their choices "stay within the legal structure" and do not infringe on the rights of other people[12]. It falls on the State to "curb any propensity or proclivity of popular sentiment or majoritarianism"[13].

While it is appropriate for the state to try to protect the established morality of a given time and location, enforcing obscenity penalties would limit an individual's choice of both voluntary and involuntary exposures to topics of dubious taste. A person's opinion cannot be shaped by state policies. Finally, it's about moral values. "Are not simply the moral convictions or mores of a particular society," but are questions of justice at the centre of morality[14]. Using constitutional morality as a principle would ensure the required uniformity while also eliminating the possibility of arbitrariness. Using the constitutional morality principle would ensure the desired uniformity while also eliminating the possibility of arbitrariness. Furthermore, when a constitutional right is limited, the reason for the limitation can be traced back to the Constitution. This line of thinking was first expressed in the Naz Foundation, and it has since resurfaced in the post-Puttaswamy period[15]. Individual autonomy has been recognised as a facet of the fundamental right to privacy, and moral values have been recast in the mould of constitutional morality[16]. The Supreme Court has agreed that constitutional morality, rather than "general morality at any moment," should govern the law[17].

[1] (2019) 3 SCC 429.

[2] *Ibid*

[3] *Ibid*

[4] Louis Henkin, Morals and the Constitution: The Sin of Obscenity, 63 Column. L. Rev. 391, 393–94 (1963) cited in Mary-Rose Papandrea, Sex and Religion: Unholy Bedfellows 116 (6) Michigan Law Review 859, 870 (2018)

[5] Lord Devlin's concept of "religious conviction" as "a degree of disgust growing to bigotry," according to Dworkin, would subject an individual's freedom to the biases and personal aversions of the majority. See Ronald Dworkin, Lord Devlin And The Enforcement Of Morals, 75 Yale L.J. 986, 988 (1965-1966).

[6] See, Andrew Ashworth, Is Criminal Law a Lost Cause 116 L.Q. Rev. 225 (2000).

[7] LatikaVashist, Re-Thinking Criminalisable Harm in India: Constitutional Morality as a Restraint on Criminalisation, 55 (1) Journal of the Indian Law Institute, 73, 92 (2013)

[8] 160 (2009) DLT 277

[9] ManojNarula v. Union of India, (2014) 9 SCC 1, 49.

[10] Government of NCT of Delhi v. Union of India and Ors. 2018 (8) SCALE 72

[11] Ajay Goswami, 2007 1 SCC 143, ¶67₁

[12] MANU/SC/0947/2018

[13] *Ibid*

[14] A. R. Blackshield, The Hart Devlin Controversy in 1965, 5 Sydney Law Review 441, 452 (1967).

[15] Navtej Singh Johar v. Union of India, (2018) 10 SCC 1; Joseph Shine v. Union of India, (2019) 3 SCC 39

[16] Joseph Shine v. Union of India, (2019) 3 SCC 39

[17] *Ibid*

CHAPTER EIGHT

CONCLUSION

It is indisputable that all civilized nations strive to advance the interest of its people by employing a variegated set of means. Criminal law is aimed at dealing with the vices of the society through the legitimate violence of the State. The ideals of criminalization that seem to be best justifying the criminalization of obscenity in Indian penal policy are a mix of legal moralism and legal paternalism. Laws prohibiting obscenity are a legal limitation on freedom of speech and expression that the State enforces for the advancement of public interest[1].

In India, the judicial trend has been to view obscenity as sexual explicitness based on its moral underpinnings. Since morality is such a nebulous concept, it must be approached with caution. The authors believe that Constitutional morality should serve as a useful guide for the judiciary in regulating obscenity in such a way that "liberty" does not become "licence" and a careful balancing of the interests of the majority and minority in society is achieved. According to Ashworth, if the descriptive, normative, and practical elements of criminal law are considered[2], the State can only use the sword of criminal law when "obscenity" exceeds a certain level. Regulation of such material without criminalization can also act as a means of social control below that level. Stripping of a person's liberty for publication of an allegedly obscene material without strongly heeding to the intent of the publisher on the ground of public morality, traced from arbitrary sources, does not go well with the constitutional spirit of Indian Constitution, and a sound application of "constitutional morality" to deal with such cases should become the guiding norm for the application of criminal law in a liberal State like India.

Obscenity changes with time, values, society, popular culture etc. The number of things that have a direct impact on the standards and level of obscenity are many and locking them into one line or a few lines is not possible.[3] To avoid the uncertainty and aberrations that currently characterise the problem, it is critical to resolve this paradigm shift and bring the law into compliance with it. The Supreme Court's recent move towards constitutional morality[4] in assessing criminalizablebehaviour is a welcome development. The apex court has sought to establish a normative framework to help in the rigorous judicial review of legislation. The constitutional courts are required to ensure that constitutional morality prevails in their judicial involvement and imagination, and that their decisions are not swayed by the tides of popular understanding of societal morality.

[1]INDIA CONST, Art 19 §, cl 2

[2]Andrew Ashworth, Is Criminal Law a Lost Cause 116 L.Q. Rev. 225 (2000)

[3]VallabhaneniVamsi Mohan, Supra note.2

[4]Navtej Singh Johar v. Union of India, (2018) 10 SCC 1; Joseph Shine v. Union of India, (2019) 3 SCC 39